When We Became Three

When **We** Became Three

A MEMORY BOOK
for THE MODERN FAMILY

JILL CARYL WEINER

PLAIN SIGHT PUBLISHING
AN IMPRINT OF CEDAR FORT, INC.
SPRINGVILLE, UT

ISBN 13: 978-1-4621-1268-5

Published by Plain Sight Publishing, an imprint of Cedar Fort, Inc.
2373 W. 700 S., Springville, UT 84663
Distributed by Cedar Fort, Inc., www.cedarfort.com

Cover and page design by Angela D. Olsen
Cover design © 2013 by Lyle Mortimer
Edited by Whitney Lindsley and Haley Miller
Author photo by Jonas Gustavsson

Printed in the United States of America

10 9 8

Contents

Congratulations!

You are an awesome new family embarking on the adventure of a lifetime. While Baby is transforming from a sleeping-eating-pooping machine to the cutest, most adorable little person ever, you're managing the bumps and burps in the road to become confident, competent parents. The adventure you're beginning belongs to three.

When We Became Three is a low-maintenance and pressure-free, wise yet whimsical way to capture all the milestones and special moments of your own special family. Within these pages, you can immortalize each incredible stage of Baby's life and celebrate your own magical milestones as new parents. It's a great activity to do with your partner and creates a wonderful, joyous keepsake that will keep you laughing, reflecting, and reminiscing for years to come.

As a new family, your lives and memories are forever intertwined. Let the pages of this book tell your story.

—Jill

How We Became Two

How We Became Two

There was a time before you were born, when Mommy and Daddy hadn't even met. It's a _____ story. It was back in _____. We met when/because _____ _____. It was a(n) _____ first meeting. The **(circle one)** funniest, most interesting, most memorable thing that happened was _____ _____. The **(circle one)** most memorable, most important, wackiest thing _____ ever said to _____ was _____ _____.

If there was one pivotal moment in our relationship, it was _____ _____.

Since we became two, a lot of _____ things have happened. We love being together because _____. We both like to _____, and _____, and our favorite times together are when _____. One great memory we have together is _____ _____. Now we're looking forward to creating more great memories with you.

WHEN WE MET IT WAS LIKE

- ☐ Fireworks—we felt sparks flying
- ☐ Castanets—we really clicked
- ☐ A soft drizzling rain—safe and comfortable
- ☐ An earthquake—what a disaster
- ☐ A Tuesday morning—nothing out of the ordinary
- ☐ Other: _____

Here's the quick version of the story: _____

_____

_____

_____

_____

_____

_____

_____

_____

_____

_____

IN THOSE EARLY DAYS

- ☐ We knew we'd be together forever.
- ☐ We started as friends, and love grew from friendship.
- ☐ We couldn't stand each other.
- ☐ One of us took an interest before the other.
- ☐ Other: _____

IF OUR RELATIONSHIP HAD A SEASON, IT WOULD BE

☐ Winter   ☐ Spring   ☐ Summer   ☐ Fall

Because: _____
_____
_____
_____

The moment Mom knew she was in love: _____
_____
_____
_____
_____
_____
_____
_____
_____

The moment Dad knew he was in love: _____
_____
_____
_____
_____
_____
_____
_____
_____

When We Were Two

"Every heart sings a song, incomplete,
until another heart whispers back."

PLATO

The 411 on Us

Our song: _____

Our favorite restaurant: _____

Our typical date: _____

_____

_____

A perfect evening we've had: _____

_____

_____

_____

A favorite outing we've had: _____

_____

_____

_____

_____

_____

_____

"I'll let you be in my dreams if I can be in yours."

BOB DYLAN

Our favorite vacation spot: _____

_____

_____

Favorite sports: _____

_____

_____

Favorite films: _____

_____

_____

Other things we like to do together: _____

_____

_____

Things we love about each other: _____

_____

_____

_____

Sweetest thing Dad ever said to Mom: _____

_____

_____

Sweetest thing Mom ever said to Dad: _____

_____

_____

Most romantic moment: _____

_____

_____

_____

Funniest moments: _____

_____

_____

_____

Scariest moments: _____

_____

_____

_____

Things we love about our relationship that we want to preserve after Baby is born: _____

_____

_____

_____

_____

_____

⏱ TIME CAPSULE

If we were making a time capsule about our relationship before Baby, we would be sure to include _____

_____

_____

_____

_____

_____

_____

_____

"Love him and let him love you. Do you think anything else under heaven really matters?"

JAMES BALDWIN

Work and Day-to-Day

We love spending the day together,
but it's not always possible.

MOM

I usually spend my days _____
_____

My dream job would be _____
_____

In my free time, I _____
_____

Something you might not know about me is _____
_____

DAD

I usually spend my days _____
_____

My dream job would be _____
_____

In my free time, I _____
_____

Something you might not know about me is _____
_____

Expecting the Unexpected

WE WANTED TO HAVE YOU

- ☐ Right away
- ☐ After a little while so we'd be ready
- ☐ Other: _____

MOM

WHAT SIGNS POINTED YOU TO TAKING A PREGNANCY TEST?

- ☐ My cycle quit cycling.
- ☐ I developed a superhero's sense of smell.
- ☐ Anything I put down came back up.
- ☐ I was too exhausted to reach for the remote.
- ☐ I felt a little too fabulous.
- ☐ Other: _____

HOW YOU FELT WHEN IT CAME BACK POSITIVE:

- ☐ Elated
- ☐ Nervous
- ☐ Complete
- ☐ Unprepared
- ☐ Energized
- ☐ Ready for the challenge
- ☐ Other:_____

How you told your partner: _____

_____

_____

His reaction: _____

_____

When and where we told our family: _____

_____

_____

_____

How we told our friends: _____

_____

_____

_____

Favorite reactions: _____

_____

_____

_____

Mom started showing at _____

Mom tried to hide it or flaunt it: _____

Details and thoughts: _____

_____

_____

_____

_____

_____

_____

Rocky Road Ice Cream
with a Side of Pickles

Food cravings: _____

_____

_____

Repulsions: _____

_____

_____

Any senses on overdrive? _____

_____

_____

_____

_____

WHICH OF THE SEVEN PREGNANT
DWARFS WERE YOU?

- ☐ Happy
- ☐ Sleepy
- ☐ Weepy
- ☐ Moody
- ☐ Hungry
- ☐ Grumpy
- ☐ Queasy
- ☐ Other: _____

Expectant Mom Adventures

Best thing about being pregnant: _____

Worst thing about being pregnant: _____

Expectant Dad Aventures

The most challenging pregnancy-related
request from Mom:

_____

_____

EXCUSES DAD USED TO AVOID
READING BABY BOOKS:

- ☐ I have to stay late at the office.
- ☐ People managed for thousands of years without Lamaze.
- ☐ The World Series, NBA Playoffs,
  Miss America contest is on.
- ☐ I have to bring the car in for its annual checkup.
- ☐ Dad read more baby books than Mom.
- ☐ Other: _____

Details and thoughts about the early
stages of pregnancy:

_____

_____

_____

_____

_____

"Love does not consist in gazing at each other but in looking together in the same direction."

BABY INVASION PREPAREDNESS CHECKLIST

- [ ] Decorate the nursery
- [ ] Take Lamaze or birthing classes
- [ ] Buy bassinet, crib, and supplies
- [ ] Pack a bag for the hospital
- [ ] Other: _____

MAKING SPACE FOR BABY

Did you create a nursery with a color and theme?

_____

Details and thoughts: _____

_____

_____

_____

Anything unusual in the hospital bag?_____

_____

Mom's biggest concerns about becoming three:

_____

_____

Dad's biggest concerns about becoming three:

_____

_____

Before you were born, we wondered or worried about

_____

_____

Gender Relations

Mom thought you'd be a _____

Dad thought you'd be a _____

- ☐ We found out your gender beforehand.
- ☐ We wanted to be surprised and waited.

What I loved about my baby shower: _____

_____

_____

_____

Who threw it and where? _____

_____

_____

Who came, and what gifts they brought for you:

_____

_____

_____

_____

Favorite gifts and memories: _____

_____

_____

_____

_____

_____

Seeing the sonogram was like _____

_____

Or we didn't get to see it because _____

_____

During the sonogram, we felt _____

_____

SONOGRAM PICTURE
OR PHOTO OF MOM'S
PREGNANT BELLY

"Always kiss your children goodnight,
even if they're already asleep."

H. JACKSON BROWN JR.

Parenting principles we agree on: _____

_____

_____

Parenting principles we're still trying to
convince each other to adopt:

_____

_____

_____

_____

ARGUMENTS WE'VE HAD:

- ☐ Baby names
- ☐ Which teams' miniature jerseys the baby will wear
- ☐ Colors for the nursery
- ☐ Whose favorite bands the baby's listening to in the womb
- ☐ Whether we need to take prep classes
- ☐ Other: _____

"Life is tough enough without having someone kick you from the inside."

RITA RUDNER

WAITING FOR YOU IS LIKE WAITING

- ☐ For cake to rise—we know you will be sweet and delicious.
- ☐ For a train—we want you to take us to our next destination.
- ☐ For a roller coaster—we can't wait for the thrill ride.
- ☐ For a hurricane—we're not sure we're prepared.
- ☐ For rain in a drought—we really want you to come already!
- ☐ Other: _____

> "The four most important words
> in any marriage: I'll do the dishes."
>
> AUTHOR UNKNOWN

The Match Made in Heaven Game

Rules: (1) Make sure you're both in an agreeable mood, and **(2)** match yourselves with your future baby-related responsibilities. Sharing is encouraged!

MOM

DAD

Sending the baby announcements

Changing diapers

Acting as baby fashion police

Reading boring parenting books

Preparing and cooking food or ordering in

Getting up at night with the baby

Doing laundry

Keeping up the family blog or photo album

Doing the dishes

Bathing Baby

Helpful advice from others about pregnancy, labor, or parenting:

_____

_____

_____

Crazy advice from others about pregnancy, labor, or parenting:

_____

_____

_____

> "Children have never been very good
> at listening to their elders, but they have
> never failed to imitate them."
>
> JAMES BALDWIN

They Bring Out the Best

 **DAD**

Personality traits you want Baby to inherit from Mom:

_____

_____

_____

Physical attributes you want Baby to inherit from Mom:

_____

_____

_____

Qualities you want Baby to inherit from you:

_____

_____

_____

_____

_____

_____

"She got her looks from her father.
He's a plastic surgeon."

GROUCHO MARX

They Bring Out the Best

MOM

Personality traits you want Baby to inherit from Dad:

_____

_____

_____

Physical attributes you want Baby to inherit from Dad:

_____

_____

_____

Qualities you want Baby to inherit from you:

_____

_____

_____

_____

_____

_____

_____

"If pregnancy were a book,
they would cut the last two chapters."

NORA EPHRON

 MOM

MEMORIES I CAN'T WAIT TO MAKE WITH BABY

1. _____

2. _____

3. _____

4. _____

5. _____

 DAD

MEMORIES I CAN'T WAIT TO MAKE WITH BABY

1. _____

2. _____

3. _____

4. _____

5. _____

Our First Letter to Baby

Date: _____

_____

_____

_____

_____

_____

_____

_____

_____

_____

_____

_____

_____

_____

_____

_____

_____

_____

_____

_____

_____

PLACE FIRST FAMILY
PHOTO HERE

You're here!

When We Became Three

When We Beame Three

On _____ , _____ this incredibly
_____ thing happened: You were born! We knew
you were coming because _____.

Mom **(circle one)** said, screamed, felt _____
_____.

Dad _____
_____.

We called _____
_____.

Here's what happened next: _____
_____
_____
_____.

When you arrived we couldn't believe _____
_____
_____
_____.

Who knew you'd be so _____!

We decided to call you _____ because
_____.

These loved ones wanted to see you right away: _____
_____
_____
_____
_____
_____.

Your being born changed our whole world. We went from two
to three. We changed from a couple to a family!

> "Giving birth is like taking your lower lip
> and forcing it over your head."
>
> CAROL BURNETT

The Labor Room:
A Judgment-Free Zone

MOM GAVE BIRTH

- ☐ At home
- ☐ In the bathtub
- ☐ At the hospital
- ☐ In the hospital elevator
- ☐ In the back of the car
- ☐ Other: _____

WHILE MOM WAS GIVING BIRTH, DAD WAS

- ☐ Hiding under the bed
- ☐ Holding Mom's hand
- ☐ Unconscious
- ☐ Praying
- ☐ Trying to find the doctor
- ☐ Other: _____

DELIVERY DOCTOR/MIDWIFE _____ WAS

- ☐ Magical
- ☐ Professional
- ☐ A linebacker
- ☐ Kind and funny
- ☐ A tough taskmaster
- ☐ Other: _____

Introducing Us!

"People are giving birth underwater now. They say it's less traumatic for the baby . . . But certainly more traumatic for the other people in the pool."

ELAYNE BOOSLER

It's a Baby!

Name: _____

Date and time of birth: _____

Location: _____

Length: _____

Weight: _____

Eye color: _ _____

Hair color: _____

Hairstyle:
☐ Fuzz   ☐ Mohawk   ☐ Cue ball   ☐ Other: _____

Details and thoughts: _____

_____

_____

_____

_____

WHEN YOU CAME OUT, YOU WERE

- ☐ Sleeping peacefully
- ☐ Bright red and bursting
- ☐ Twisting and shouting
- ☐ Calmly looking around
- ☐ Absolutely beautiful
- ☐ Other: _____

BABY LOOKS LIKE (CHECK ALL THAT APPLY)

- ☐ Yoda (only cuter)
- ☐ A perfect baby doll
- ☐ Grandma or Grandpa
- ☐ Mom
- ☐ Dad
- ☐ Other: _____

ADD A PHOTO
OF BABY

"A new baby is like the beginning of all things—wonder, hope, a dream of possibilities."

EDA J. LeSHAN

It's a Mom!

Name: _____

Besides "Best Mom Ever," circle the name you hope Baby will call you:

Mom   Mama   Mommy   Ma'am

Madre   Mami   Other: _____

Birth date: _____

Zodiac sign: _____

Height in heels or flats: _____

Weight gained during pregnancy: _____

Hair color at the time: _____

ADD A PHOTO
OF MOM

> "A father is someone who carries
> pictures where his money used to be."
>
> AUTHOR UNKNOWN

It's a Dad!

Name: _____

Besides "Best Dad Ever," circle the name
you hope Baby will call you:

Dad   Daddy   Dada   Pop   Papa

Poppy   Sir   Coach   Other: _____

Birth date: _____

Zodiac sign: _____

Height in dreams (or reality): _____

Hair: ☐ Yes   ☐ No   ☐ On its way out

> "When he lay on my chest for the first time, part of me felt as if someone had given me a Martian baby. . . . The other part of me felt like I was holding my own soul."

ANNE LAMOTT

It's a Mom!

MY FEELINGS UPON SEEING
YOU FOR THE FIRST TIME:

- [ ] Love
- [ ] Fear
- [ ] Pride
- [ ] Awe
- [ ] Joy
- [ ] Relief
- [ ] Other: _____

WHEN I FIRST SAW YOU I
(CHECK AS MANY AS APPLY)

- [ ] Wept
- [ ] Kissed Dad
- [ ] Wanted to hold you more than anything
- [ ] Smiled like a fool
- [ ] Freaked out
- [ ] Other: _____

THE FIRST TIME I HELD YOU, YOU WERE

- ☐ Sleeping like an angel
- ☐ Wriggling like a worm
- ☐ Curious and looking around
- ☐ Comfortable in my arms
- ☐ Crying inconsolably
- ☐ Other: _____

Any words to Baby and Dad as well as details and thoughts from that special day:

_____

_____

_____

_____

_____

_____

_____

_____

_____

_____

_____

_____

_____

_____

_____

*"If you think my hands are full,
you should see my heart!"*

A PROUD FATHER

It's a Dad!

MY FEELINGS UPON SEEING
YOU FOR THE FIRST TIME:

- ☐ Relief
- ☐ Awe
- ☐ Fear
- ☐ Joy
- ☐ Love
- ☐ Pride
- ☐ Other: _____

WHEN I FIRST SAW YOU I
(CHECK AS MANY AS APPLY)

- ☐ Wept
- ☐ Kissed Mom
- ☐ Wanted to hold you
- ☐ Smiled like a fool
- ☐ Freaked out
- ☐ Cut the umbilical cord

THE FIRST TIME I HELD YOU, YOU WERE

☐ In a perfect, peaceful sleep
☐ Writhing like you'd jump out of my arms
☐ Turning colors like a chameleon
☐ Comfortable in my arms
☐ Crying inconsolably
☐ Other: _____

Any words to Baby and Mom as well as details and thoughts from that special day:

_____

_____

_____

_____

_____

_____

_____

_____

_____

_____

_____

_____

_____

_____

_____

Hindsight Is 20/20:
The Dos and Don'ts of Childbirth

THINGS TO REMEMBER FOR NEXT TIME

😊 MOM

- [ ] Bean burritos do not make a good pre-delivery meal.
- [ ] Breathe.
- [ ] Pack slippers and snacks and have bag ready.
- [ ] Don't worry if Dad faints—other people will help.
- [ ] Don't invite the immediate world to come over the next day.
- [ ] Other: _____

😊 DAD

- [ ] I'm supposed to act calm.
- [ ] Make sure to have gas in the car and the bag packed.
- [ ] Carry mints: Mom and I get very close.
- [ ] Carry favorite snacks for a long delivery.
- [ ] Don't leave Mom at home in my rush to the hospital.
- [ ] Other: _____

What do you wish you had done differently? _____

_____

_____

What aspects were absolutely perfect? _____

_____

_____

"Lions and tigers and bears. Oh my!"

DOROTHY IN *THE WIZARD OF OZ*

BABY FEATURE MATCH

	Mom's	Dad's	Who Knows?
Eyes			
Nose			
Mouth			
Smile			
Head shape			
Ears			
Fingers			
Feet			

IF YOU WERE A BABY ANIMAL, YOU WOULD BE

☐ A piranha—always eating and sniping at Mom
☐ A koala—cuddly and always snoozing
☐ A puppy—joyous and mischievous
☐ A howler monkey—constantly wailing
☐ Other: _____

Details and thoughts: _____

_____

_____

_____

_____

_____

_____

"A rose by any other name would smell as sweet."

Baby's Name

We named you _____

because _____

_____.

Names we liked but couldn't agree on: _____

_____

_____

Silliest names we considered: _____

_____

_____

If you had been the opposite gender, we would have named you: _____

_____

_____.

We might call you _____ as a nickname.

What we called you before you were born: _____

_____

Notes or stories: _____

_____

_____

_____

_____.

Parents' Names

Mom was named _____

because _____

_____

_____.

Nicknames she's had: _____

_____

_____

Dad was named _____

because _____

_____

_____.

Nicknames he's had: _____

_____

_____

_____

NEW IMPORTANT NAMES:

Pediatrician: _____

Babysitters: _____

_____

Godparents: _____

_____

Favorite takeout restaurant: _____

"If nothing is going well, call your grandmother."

Our Family, Our Village

FIRST FAMILY VISITORS

These loved ones live close and love to come see you.
Babysitting, anyone? _____

_____

_____

These loved ones live far away but send
you all their love:

_____

_____

_____

We wish these loved ones were still with us: _____

_____

_____

"It's the friends you can call up at 4 a.m. that matter."

MARLENE DIETRICH

These friends are like family: _____

_____

_____

_____

_____

_____

Bringing Baby Home

WHEN WE LEFT THE HOSPITAL, WE

- ☐ Were thrilled beyond belief
- ☐ Felt exhausted and in need of care
- ☐ Couldn't believe they let us leave with you
- ☐ Were worried you might break
- ☐ Felt unprepared and clueless
- ☐ Were crazy nervous yet ecstatic
- ☐ Other: _____

Stories or memories: _____

_____

_____

_____

_____

_____

WHEN WE FIRST STEPPED INSIDE OUR HOME WITH
YOU, WE KNEW EVERYTHING HAD

- ☐ Changed
- ☐ CHANGED!
- ☐ Other: _____

First address: _____

Why it will always be special: _____

_____

_____

_____

"Before I got married I had six theories
about bringing up children; now
I have six children and no theories."

JOHN WILMOT

The biggest challenge: _____
_____
_____
_____

The greatest triumph: _____
_____
_____
_____

The biggest adjustment: _____
_____
_____
_____

Silliest things we did as nervous new parents: _____
_____
_____
_____

Details and thoughts: _____
_____
_____
_____
_____

Baby's First Month/Parents' First Daze

Baby's First Month/ Parents' First Daze

(YOU CAN COME BACK TO THIS AFTER YOU FILL OUT THE CHAPTER.)

Bringing you home was absolutely _____.

I mean, it's not every day you step through your door knowing your life has changed forever. Just a few days before this, we were _____ and all of a sudden we're _____.

We thought we'd have a lot to teach you, but we immediately realized we had a lot to learn. You were so _____ and we were so _____. We felt so _____ _____.

Sometimes, all you seemed to want to do was _____ and all we wanted to do was _____. The biggest surprise was _____!

But it's so worth it. Your _____ is the most adorable thing on the planet! Sure, taking care of a newborn can be tricky, especially _____ _____,

but we're working everything out together. We hate to brag, but already we're really good at _____ _____.

We feel so lucky and _____ that you're part of our family. Being three is just where we want to be.

All you need is love (and food,
and diaper changes, and a ton of sleep).

Baby's First Month

NOW THAT YOU'RE HOME,
WE'RE SURPRISED ABOUT

- [ ] How beautiful you are
- [ ] How truly dependent you are
- [ ] How much you sleep
- [ ] How much you eat
- [ ] How tricky it is to feed you
- [ ] How easy it is feed you
- [ ] Other: _____

Details and thoughts: _____

_____

_____

_____

_____

_____

_____

_____

WE ALWAYS WANT TO REMEMBER

- [ ] How new everything feels
- [ ] That you once fit in the crook of our arms
- [ ] How soft your skin feels
- [ ] That these days are exhausting but
  amazing at the same time
- [ ] Other: _____

Parents' First Daze

WHILE YOU WERE LEARNING ABOUT THE WORLD,
WE WERE LEARNING TO CARE FOR ALL YOUR NEEDS

When you first came home, Mom felt _____

_____

_____

_____

These first days, Dad felt _____

_____

_____

_____

Details and thoughts: _____

_____

_____

_____

_____

Like a dream from your heart,
these days will remain fuzzy.

WE ADORE YOUR

- ☐ Puffy cheeks
- ☐ Tiny lips
- ☐ Abundant thighs
- ☐ Perfectly curled eyelashes
- ☐ Petal-soft skin
- ☐ Not to mention: _____

Besides how you look physically, we love _____
_____

_____

WE'RE REALLY AMAZED

- ☐ By your perfect fingers
- ☐ By your chiseled toes
- ☐ By your numerous poops
- ☐ By your sparkling eyes
- ☐ That we made something so beautiful
- ☐ Other: _____

It's incredible that just a few days ago we were _____
_____

_____

And now we're _____
_____

_____

And it's amazing that you're _____
_____

_____

We started calling you _____
_____

_____

WE'D DESCRIBE YOU AS

- ☐ Sleeping beauty
- ☐ Screaming beauty
- ☐ A vacuum cleaner
- ☐ A power pooper
- ☐ A stealth pooper
- ☐ A little love bug
- ☐ Other: _____

YOU'RE PRACTICALLY PERFECT IN EVERY WAY.
NOW IF ONLY YOU WOULD

- [ ] Eat more
- [ ] Eat less
- [ ] Sleep more
- [ ] Sleep less
- [ ] Other: _____

Comments: _____

_____

_____

_____

_____

WE'D DESCRIBE OURSELVES AS

- [ ] Sleep-deprived zombies
- [ ] Nervous nellies not quite sure what to do
- [ ] Surfer-dudes going with the flow
- [ ] Teens, giddy in love
- [ ] Like scientists tracking meals, poops, and sleep
- [ ] Like astronomers who found a new universe of love
- [ ] Other: _____

Even so, we are surprisingly good at _____

_____

_____

_____

_____

This parenting stuff would be a cinch if it wasn't for

_____

_____

_____

_____

Baby's First Meals

THIS HOLD IS BABY'S FAVORITE FOR NURSING,
TAKING A BOTTLE, ETC. (MARK ALL THAT APPLY):

- ☐ Cradle hold
- ☐ Cross-cradle hold
- ☐ Football hold
- ☐ Lying down, side-armed
- ☐ In a lap
- ☐ All of the above
- ☐ Other: _____

BABY'S EATING STYLE:

- ☐ Gorging
- ☐ Grazing
- ☐ Graze, nod off, graze, nod off
- ☐ Finicky—no thanks, maybe later
- ☐ Speed eating then spitting up all over
- ☐ Other: _____

STRATEGIES FOR KEEPING YOU
AWAKE DURING FEEDINGS:

- ☐ Tickle your feet
- ☐ Open up the windows
- ☐ Make lots of noise
- ☐ Baby's always awake during feedings
- ☐ Peel off your onesie so the cool air will wake you
- ☐ Other: _____

Favorite spit-up story: _____
_____
_____
_____

Details, thoughts, and feelings about feeding Baby:
_____
_____
_____

Baby in Dreamland

WHEN YOU SLEEP, WE WONDER

- ☐ How long it will be before you wake up
- ☐ What you're dreaming about
- ☐ How you could go from a deep sleep to wide awake and screaming in seconds
- ☐ If we'll ever know that peaceful feeling of sleep again
- ☐ Other: _____

Your favorite spot for a snooze: _____
_____
_____

Some difficulties about your sleeping: _____
_____
_____
_____
_____

Details and thoughts: _____
_____
_____
_____
_____
_____
_____
_____
_____
_____
_____
_____

Weirdest place Baby's ever fallen asleep: _____

_____

_____

_____

_____

Longest stretch that Baby slept: _____

_____

_____

_____

_____

Parents' Dreams of Dreaming

Are you able to fall back asleep after getting up with Baby? Who usually gets up, or do you take turns?

_____

_____

_____

_____

_____

_____

_____

With a regular night's sleep pretty much out the window, what's your new favorite place to curl up and nap?

_____

_____

_____

_____

*"A baby is a loud noise at one end and no sense
of responsibility at the other."*

RONALD KNOX

Diaper Drama

LEARNED THE HARD WAY

- [ ] Diapers can be explosive
- [ ] When changing, either cover or point baby boys down
- [ ] Diapers are not leak proof
- [ ] Always carry at least 4 diapers and extra clothes
- [ ] Other: _____

Any funny diaper surprises? _____
_____
_____
_____
_____

Most challenging place to change a diaper: _____
_____
_____

Do you use the word "poopy"? _____
_____
_____

QUICK-THINKING PARENTS

You used up all the diapers and Baby's dirty again. What
do you do? _____
_____
_____
_____

Diaper Etiquette

WHEN CHANGING A DIAPER AT SOMEONE ELSE'S HOUSE, WHAT DO YOU DO?

☐ Ask what to do with dirty diaper
☐ Throw it in their garbage without asking
☐ Take it home with you

DADDY DOES DIAPERS?

☐ Of course
☐ Sometimes
☐ Never

More diaper-related stories: _____

_____

_____

_____

_____

_____

_____

_____

_____

_____

_____

_____

_____

_____

_____

_____

_____

_____

Parenting Survival Skills

FOR YOU, BEING SWADDLED

☐ Feels safe like the womb
☐ Feels constricting like a straightjacket
☐ Is no big deal either way

Things we do to quiet you down: _____
_____
_____
_____
_____
_____
_____

TOUGHEST THINGS ABOUT BEING NEW PARENTS

RANK THEM FROM BAD TO WORST

☐ Explosive diapers
☐ Projectile spit-up
☐ The built-in baby alarm clock
☐ Trying to soothe an inconsolable newborn
☐ Wrestling you into diapers or swaddling blankets
☐ Other: _____
☐ Other: _____

WHAT'S WORSE?

☐ Running out of diapers when you're out
☐ Having to nurse in a public place
☐ Other: _____

Top Ten Reasons
WE LOVE BEING YOUR PARENTS

1. _____

2. _____

3. _____

4. _____

5. _____

6. _____

7. _____

8. _____

9. _____

10. _____

Baby Olympics

IN MARATHON SLEEPING, YOU WIN

- ☐ **Gold:** Smashed record by sleeping past 5:00 a.m.
- ☐ **Silver:** Beat previous 4 hours of sleep
- ☐ **Bronze:** Slept in the car seat until we reached the next state
- ☐ Didn't qualify

IN SPEED SLEEPING, YOU WIN

- ☐ **Gold:** Head pops up as soon as it goes down
- ☐ **Silver:** Does thirty seconds even count as a nap?
- ☐ **Bronze:** Set a personal record with ____ hours straight
- ☐ Didn't qualify

IN MARATHON NURSING, YOU WIN

- ☐ **Gold:** Managed to nurse almost nonstop for ____ hours
- ☐ **Silver:** You didn't stop until Mom pried you off
- ☐ **Bronze:** Stopped nursing long enough to take a 20-minute nap
- ☐ Didn't qualify

IN OLYMPIC CRYING, YOU WIN

- ☐ **Gold:** Your first days you screamed nonstop
- ☐ **Silver:** Nothing seems to soothe you
- ☐ **Bronze:** You stopped crying to eat
- ☐ Didn't qualify

IN POWER POOPING, YOU WIN

- [ ] **Gold:** We changed ____ diapers in one day
- [ ] **Silver:** As soon as your diaper was changed, you soiled the new one
- [ ] **Bronze:** What can we say, your system works
- [ ] Didn't qualify

IN DIARRHEA DIRTY DIAPER DASH, YOU WIN

- [ ] **Gold:** Leaked through diaper and clothes
- [ ] **Silver:** Soiled the new, clean diaper while it was going on
- [ ] **Bronze:** Waited until the new clean diaper was on to poop
- [ ] Didn't qualify

IN LONG-DISTANCE SPIT-UP, YOU WIN

- [ ] **Gold:** Spit-up sprayed into the living room and around the corner
- [ ] **Silver:** Reached across the kitchen
- [ ] **Bronze:** Splattered on Mom's new outfit
- [ ] Didn't qualify

IN LONG-DISTANCE STARVING, YOU WIN

- [ ] **Gold:** Refused to nurse or take a bottle
- [ ] **Silver:** Fell asleep as soon as you latched on
- [ ] **Bronze:** You spit up everything you ate
- [ ] Didn't qualify

> *"Bath time can be precious, but
> it can also be a big mess."*
>
> AUTHOR UNKNOWN

Baby's First Baths

Baby's first sponge bath: _____
_____
_____
_____

The best thing about bath time: _____
_____
_____

BATH TIME IS

- ☐ A great time to bond with Baby
- ☐ A harrowing experience
- ☐ It depends on the day

Baby Bath Happiness Meter

😊	You would rather tear your eyes out.
😊 😊	You scream for a minute and then calm down.
😊 😊 😊	You are hesitant but have a good time.
😊 😊 😊 😊	You jump out of our arms to get in.

Challenges, toys, equipment, stories: _____
_____
_____
_____
_____

ADD A PHOTO OF
BABY AT BATH TIME

Parents' Post-Baby Hygiene

When do you find the time to shower? _____

_____

_____

Challenges: _____

_____

_____

_____

_____

_____

Parental Stinky Meter

☺	You shower every day.
☺ ☺	You shower every other day.
☺ ☹ ☹	You shower every third day.
☺ ☹ ☹ ☹	You shower every week.
☹ ☹ ☹ ☹ ☹	You use a lot of perfume or cologne.

Keep Calm and Carry On: Firsts You'll Want to Forget

BABY'S FIRST PROJECTILE

☐ Poop

☐ Spit-up

Any stories? _____

_____

_____

_____

_____

Baby's first boo-boo: _____

_____

_____

_____

_____

Baby's first fever: _____

_____

_____

_____

_____

Mom and Dad's first big worries: _____

_____

_____

_____

_____

_____

First Fears

WE WERE SO NERVOUS THAT WE OFTEN

- ☐ Called the pediatrician in a panic
- ☐ Checked to see if Baby was breathing
- ☐ Called (or almost called) Poison Control

Any stories? _____

_____

_____

_____

_____

_____

_____

Who is the family worrywart? Mom or Dad? _____

DID YOU EVER THINK BABY WAS

- ☐ Starving?
- ☐ Dying?
- ☐ Choking?
- ☐ Other? _____

What was really happening? _____

_____

_____

_____

_____

_____

_____

_____

Baby's Firsts/
Parents' Firsts

Baby's Firsts/Parents' Firsts

Every day with you has a new first. First, you're so _____.
It's thrilling to watch you grow and change. It seems like every
minute you get better at _____.
When you smile at us, we _____.

Your _____ personality is shining through. We can't
help but _____ when you _____.

We will never forget the first time you _____.
One of your favorite things to do is _____,
and you're really attached to _____
_____. Mommy loves _____
with you and Daddy loves _____ with you.
You love repetition and sometimes you want us to
_____ nonstop. In fact, we've set the record for
number of times _____.

You are developing in every way and we are developing rituals.
You don't always want to _____, so the way we
get you to do it is by _____
_____.

Your first baby friends are _____
_____.

(and they are our new friends too). We love these early days of
learning and growing with you!

"A smile is the universal language of kindness."

WILLIAM ARTHUR WARD

Baby's First Smile

Where were we and how long did it last? _____
_____
_____

THAT SMILE

- ☐ Took us by surprise
- ☐ Swept us off our feet
- ☐ Nearly caused a stampede of cooing grandmas at the market
- ☐ Made us feel even more connected to you
- ☐ Gets you free lollipops wherever we go
- ☐ Other: _____

Baby's ticklish spots: _____
_____
_____

The things that make you smile or laugh are _____
_____
_____

Parents' Smile

You make Mom smile when _____
_____
_____

You make Dad smile when _____
_____
_____

> "When I was born, I was so surprised
> I didn't talk for a year and a half."
>
> GRACIE ALLEN

Baby Squawk, Baby Talk

YOU LET US KNOW WHAT YOU WANT BY

- ☐ Screaming
- ☐ Pointing
- ☐ Laughing
- ☐ Crying
- ☐ Throwing a tantrum
- ☐ Babbling
- ☐ Using baby sign language
- ☐ Other: _____

Details and thoughts: _____

_____

_____

_____

_____

_____

_____

_____

_____

_____

_____

_____

_____

_____

_____

_____

Creative Communication

WE COMMUNICATE WITH YOU WITH

- ☐ Smiles
- ☐ Cuddles
- ☐ Talking
- ☐ Baby talk
- ☐ Pointing
- ☐ Sign language
- ☐ Inflection in our voices
- ☐ Other: _____

FAST FORWARD: IN THE FUTURE, HOW WILL YOU COMMUNICATE THINGS TO EACH OTHER THAT YOU DON'T WANT BABY TO UNDERSTAND?

- ☐ Pig Latin
- ☐ Spelling
- ☐ We speak _____
- ☐ Sign language
- ☐ Other: _____

ADD A PHOTO
OF BABY

Baby's First Silly Sounds

YOU'RE

☐ A bubbler
☐ A babbler
☐ A raspberry blower
☐ The strong, silent type
☐ Other: _____

Your first sounds: _____
_____
_____
_____

Describe: _____
_____
_____
_____

Bubble Meter

◯	You never blow bubbles
◯◯	Once in a while a bubble will grow
◯◯◯	Moderately bubbly to loud raspberries
◯◯◯◯	A raspberry smoothie
◯◯◯◯◯	You're a regular bubble machine

SOCIAL BUTTERFLY? TRUE OR FALSE

T/F   You love blowing kisses.
T/F   You love waving bye-bye.
T/F   You sing baby songs.
T/F   You're a natural at patty cake.
T/F   You really don't like to perform.

Parents' First Baby Sounds

SOMETIMES WE'RE SILLY AND
COMMUNICATE WITH YOU BY

- ☐ Talking and pointing
- ☐ Blowing bubbles
- ☐ Making raspberries on your belly
- ☐ Tickling you
- ☐ Mimicking your sounds
- ☐ Making sounds for you to mimic
- ☐ Laughing with you
- ☐ Singing to you
- ☐ Other: _____

Which of the above does Baby like the best? _____

_____

_____

_____

Details and thoughts: _____

_____

_____

_____

_____

_____

_____

_____

_____

_____

_____

_____

_____

Baby's First Real Words

First time you said "dada": _____
_____
_____
_____

First time you said "mama": _____
_____
_____
_____

Your words with lost letters (like "poon" instead of spoon):
_____
_____
_____

Your first and favorite words and expressions: _____
_____
_____
_____

BABY'S FIRST WORDS FOR

Mom: _____

Dad: _____

Milk: _____

Bottle: _____

Water: _____

Blanket: _____

Binkie: _____

Favorite toy: _____

Grandma or Grandpa: _____

"I can't find bubu's ba-ba!"

Parents' First Baby Words

Mama's first baby words: _____
_____
_____
_____

Dada's first baby words: _____
_____
_____
_____

Parents' first baby words to each other: _____
_____
_____
_____
_____

Do you call each other silly pet names, or do baby words
ever slip into your conversations? _____
_____
_____
_____
_____

How does it feel calling your partner Daddy or Mommy?
(Or do you call them something else instead?)
_____
_____
_____
_____
_____

Baby's First Friends

THE 411 ON FRIENDSHIP

Your first friends were _____
_____
_____
_____
_____

This is how you met: _____
_____
_____
_____
_____

Your favorite things to do with friends are _____
_____
_____
_____
_____
_____
_____

ADD A PHOTO OF
BABY AND A FRIEND

> "Friendship is born at that moment when one person says to another: 'What! You too? I thought I was the only one.'"
>
> C.S. LEWIS

Parents' First Baby-Related Friends

Who are they and where did you meet? _____
_____
_____
_____
_____

Great memories with new friends: _____
_____
_____
_____
_____

These old friends also have little babies or are having them soon: _____
_____
_____

Details and thoughts: _____
_____
_____
_____
_____
_____
_____
_____

"My bed is like a little boat;
Nurse tucks me in when we embark."

FIRST SITTERS OR NANNIES

- [ ] We need someone great to take care
  of you while we're at work.
- [ ] We just need someone to watch you occasionally
  when we need a night out.
- [ ] We wouldn't leave you with anyone else for now.
- [ ] Other: _____

What we're looking for in a sitter for you: _____

_____

_____

_____

_____

_____

_____

_____

_____

DEAL BREAKERS

- [ ] Texts during interview
- [ ] Chain-smokes
- [ ] Drinks "Diet Coke" out of a paper bag
- [ ] Keeps nodding off
- [ ] Winks at your partner
- [ ] Is barely out of diapers him- or herself
- [ ] Other: _____

Sometimes It Takes a Village;
Sometimes a Skillful Nanny.

Top Three Favorite Sitters and Why We Love Them

1. _____
   _____
   _____

2. _____
   _____
   _____

3. _____
   _____
   _____

If only _____ was here to babysit.

Going rate for babysitters/nannies: _____

Details and thoughts: _____
_____
_____
_____
_____
_____
_____
_____
_____
_____
_____
_____
_____
_____

Baby's First Meals

Is Mommy's milk Baby's sole nourishment?_____

FEEDING POSITION FOR BABY
NOW THAT YOU'RE A PRO

- ☐ Cradle hold
- ☐ Cross-cradle hold
- ☐ Football hold
- ☐ Lying down, side-armed
- ☐ All of the above
- ☐ Other: _____

Thoughts on feeding: _____

_____

_____

_____

Baby's Nutritional Plate

Baby's First Bottle

COULD BE BREAST MILK, WATER, OR FORMULA

Date: _____

GETTING YOU TO TAKE A BOTTLE WAS

- ☐ Like forcing a vegetarian to eat worms
- ☐ As easy as giving hugs
- ☐ You never took a bottle

Parents' Meal Plan

WHAT'S YOUR GO-TO MEAL PLAN WHEN YOU'RE
SLEEP DEPRIVED, TIME STARVED, AND HUNGRY?

☐ Toast

☐ Takeout

☐ Cereal—what kind? _____

☐ Friends helped

☐ Cooking _____

☐ Other: _____

Parents' Nutritional Plate

FILL IN THE BLANKS WITH WHAT YOU'RE EATING.
BELOW ARE A FEW OPTIONS TO CHOOSE FROM.

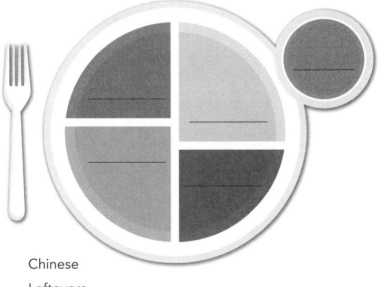

Chinese

Leftovers

Cereal

Fluids

Baby food

Whatever we can find in the fridge

"Food, glorious food!"

FROM *OLIVER!*

Baby's First Solid Food:

When? _____

What? _____

YOU WERE LIKE

☐ **Papa Bear:** Feed me! More! Faster!
☐ **Mama Bear:** Okay, I'll give it a try.
☐ **Baby Bear:** Yuck! Get that stuff away from me!
☐ Other: _____

Details and thoughts:

_____

_____

_____

_____

_____

_____

_____

_____

_____

_____

_____

_____

_____

Watch Mommy!

Parents' first mushy food: _____
_____
_____

What did you eat and why? Did you like it enough to get seconds? _____
_____
_____

What's the most disgusting baby food you've tasted? Did you feel guilty making Baby eat it after that?
_____
_____

Any baby foods you're grooving on? _____
_____
_____

Details and thoughts: _____
_____
_____
_____
_____

ADD A PHOTO OF
BABY EATING

Baby Whines and Dines

YOU LIKE

☐ Acorn squash   ☐ Pears

☐ Applesauce   ☐ Peas

☐ Apricots   ☐ Plums

☐ Avocado   ☐ Rice cereal

☐ Bananas   ☐ Sweet potatoes

☐ Barley cereal   ☐ Yellow squash

☐ Oat cereal

Others: _____

_____

_____

_____

_____

_____

You hate _____

_____

_____

_____

_____

Allergies or possible allergies: _____

_____

_____

_____

_____

"Just don't call me late for dinner."

AUTHOR UNKNOWN

Parents' Tricks and Treats

Favorite baby-friendly restaurant(s): _____

_____

_____

Tricks that got Baby to eat: _____

_____

_____

_____

_____

Tricks that backfired and turned the kitchen into a disaster area: _____

_____

_____

_____

_____

Eating fun or horror stories: _____

_____

_____

_____

_____

Any food-related tantrums, faux pas, or funny stories?

_____

_____

_____

_____

Baby's First Nights

YOU CAN'T GET TO SLEEP UNLESS

- ☐ Mom or Dad rocks you for hours
- ☐ Someone cuddles up with you
- ☐ Mom nurses you
- ☐ Someone sings to you
- ☐ You're in your car seat
- ☐ We drive you around the neighborhood
- ☐ Other: _____

ADD A PHOTO OF
BABY SLEEPING

> "People who say they sleep like a baby
> usually don't have one."
>
> LEO J. BURKE

Parents' Long Nights

Sleep Meter

😴   What is sleep?

😴 😴   Sleep is overrated.

😴 😴 😴   I'll sleep when you go to kindergarten.

😴 😴 😴 😴   I make up for lost sleep with ten-minute naps.

😴 😴 😴 😴 😴   Haven't lost a wink.

IF WE WERE WRITING A BOOK ABOUT YOUR SLEEP HABITS, THE TITLE WOULD BE

- ☐ *Long Night's Journey into Night*

- ☐ *Sleep Is a Many-Splendored Thing*

- ☐ *Night of the Living Dead*

- ☐ *I Got Up the Last 9 Times; It's Your Turn*

- ☐ *Sleepless in Seattle*

Baby's First Bedtime Rituals

YOUR BEDTIME ROUTINE INCLUDES

- ☐ Sponge bath
- ☐ Cuddling
- ☐ Nursing
- ☐ Singing
- ☐ Massage
- ☐ Reading
- ☐ Other: _____

We put you down for bed by _____

_____

_____

Your favorite part of bedtime is _____

_____

_____

_____

_____

Our favorite part of bedtime is _____

_____

_____

_____

_____

Earliest favorite stories or lullabies: _____

_____

_____

_____

_____

"The best cure for insomnia is to get a lot of sleep."

Parents' First Bedtime Rituals

Baby's finally in bed. What do you do? _____

_____

_____

_____

BEFORE GOING TO BED, YOU

- ☐ Have dinner together
- ☐ Chat
- ☐ Watch TV
- ☐ Just crash
- ☐ Other: _____

Sleep strategies for Baby: Are Mom and Dad
on the same page? _____

_____

_____

_____

_____

_____

	Mom Likes	Dad Likes
Comforting you to help you sleep		
Have Baby self-soothe		
A mixture of both		
Other: _____		

"The joys of motherhood are never fully experienced until the children are in bed."

AUTHOR UNKNOWN

THE FIRST TIME YOU SLEPT THROUGH THE NIGHT, WE THOUGHT

- ☐ It was a freak accident
- ☐ It was a miracle
- ☐ We were in the wrong house
- ☐ Time to celebrate! We could finally get back to a normal schedule (yeah, right)
- ☐ Something was wrong with you and called the pediatrician
- ☐ Other: _____

WHILE YOU SLEPT THROUGH YOUR FIRST NIGHT, MOM

- ☐ Checked to see if you were breathing
- ☐ Tried to watch TV
- ☐ Lay awake staring at the ceiling
- ☐ Slept peacefully
- ☐ Stayed up with Dad worrying that she should call 911
- ☐ Other: _____

WHILE YOU SLEPT, DAD

- ☐ Checked to see if you were breathing
- ☐ Watched sports
- ☐ Snoozed on the couch as usual
- ☐ Slept peacefully
- ☐ Lay awake staring at the ceiling
- ☐ Stayed up with Mom waiting for Baby to wake up
- ☐ Other: _____

Somebody Pinch Me!

First time Mom slept through the night (without checking
to see if Baby was alive): _____
_____

Did you have trouble sleeping through the night the first
time Baby slept through the night? If so, why? _____
_____

Details and thoughts: _____
_____
_____
_____

First time Dad slept through the night: _____
_____

Was this a big deal or a usual thing? _____
_____

Details and thoughts: _____
_____
_____
_____

Baby's First Steps
toward Independence

HOLDING HEAD UP
Details: _____
_____

WAVING BYE-BYE / BLOWING KISSES
Details: _____
_____

SITTING UP
Details: _____
_____

ROLLING OVER
Details: _____
_____

CRAWLING
Details:_____
_____

Style: ☐ Traditional ☐ Backward ☐ Belly ☐ Other: _____

CRUISING
Details: _____
_____
_____
_____
_____

Favorite thing to cruise on: _____

Parents' Baby Steps
in Adjusting to a New Life

HOLDING HEAD UP WHILE COVERED WITH SPIT-UP:

- ☐ No problem, we've got a baby
- ☐ Help! Where's a change of clothes?
- ☐ Lesson aearned: always use a burp cloth

WAVING BYE-BYE WHEN YOU NEED
TO GO TO WORK OR JUST OUT:

- ☐ One of the hardest parts of parenting
- ☐ We know that the baby will be fine
  once we're out the door

ROLLING OVER TO GO BACK TO SLEEP

Our system or schedule for getting up with you at night:

_____

_____

_____

_____

_____

_____

_____

_____

_____

"The journey of a thousand miles
begins with a single step."

LAO-TZU

Baby's First Step

Who was there to witness? _____

When was it? _____

Where were we? _____

IT WAS

☐ A lone step and a crash
☐ A few steps and a carefully planned fall
☐ An awkward dance across the floor
☐ A flawless journey front point A to B
☐ Spectacular
☐ Other or describe in your own words: _____

BABY WAS

☐ Thrilled
☐ Glad when it was over
☐ Surprised
☐ Uninterested
☐ Other: _____

When did Baby really start walking? _____

_____

Details and thoughts: _____

_____

_____

Parents' First Step Out of the House without Baby

MOM

Where did you go? _____

YOU WANTED TO

- ☐ Call home immediately
- ☐ Make a break for the border
- ☐ Rush back to check on Baby
- ☐ Something in between
- ☐ Stay close by just in case
- ☐ Other (describe): _____

_____

Details, thoughts, and emotions: _____

_____

_____

DAD

Where did you go? _____

YOU WANTED TO

- ☐ Call home immediately
- ☐ Make a break for the border
- ☐ Rush back to check on Baby
- ☐ Something in between
- ☐ Put on a disguise and sneak back home
- ☐ Other (describe): _____

_____

Details, thoughts, and emotions: _____

_____

_____

One small step for baby,
one giant leap for independence.

Baby's First Trip Out of the House without Parents

Who did you go with? _____

_____

Where did you go? _____

_____

What did you do? _____

_____

How long were you gone? _____

You were _____ old.

Details: _____

_____

_____

_____

_____

_____

_____

Parents' First Step Out of the House Together without Baby

Where did you go and how long were you out? _____

_____

_____

Who watched Baby? _____

_____

_____

How did you feel about leaving Baby behind? _____

_____

_____

_____

_____

Did you wind up talking about Baby the whole time?

_____

_____

_____

_____

_____

Baby's First Tantrum

When and where: _____

_____

_____

What caused it? _____

_____

_____

_____

_____

_____

How did Mom/Dad handle it? _____

_____

_____

_____

_____

_____

_____

_____

_____

_____

"All of us have moments in our lives that test our courage. Taking children into a house with a white carpet is one of them. "

ERMA BOMBECK

Parents' First Tantrum

Mom lost her cool when _____
_____
_____
_____

Afterward, Mom (did, thought, said, wanted) _____
_____
_____
_____

Dad lost his cool when _____
_____
_____
_____

Afterward, Dad (did, thought, said, wanted) _____
_____
_____
_____

> "A perfect example of minority rule
> is a baby in the house."

AUTHOR UNKNOWN

Baby Tantrum Prevention

Warning signs that you were going to have a tantrum:

_____

_____

_____

You're most likely to lose it in these situations: _____

_____

_____

_____

OUR PREVENTION STRATEGIES

- ☐ Change the subject
- ☐ Pull out a lollipop
- ☐ Jiggle keys or another distraction
- ☐ Sing
- ☐ Resort to electronics
- ☐ Other: _____

Your name when you're in trouble: _____

_____

Your terrible twos really started _____

_____

> "Love does not begin and end the way
> we seem to think it does. Love is a battle,
> love is a war; love is growing up."

JAMES BALDWIN

Parent Tantrum Prevention

What pushes Mom's buttons? _____

_____

_____

How can you prevent it? _____

_____

_____

What pushes Dad's buttons? _____

_____

_____

Is there a way to prevent it? _____

_____

_____

WHAT STRATEGIES DO YOU USE TO KEEP CALM?

- ☐ Count to ten
- ☐ Sing the alphabet
- ☐ Tear out your hair
- ☐ Leave the room
- ☐ Get angry now, keep calm later

Hair today, gone tomorrow.

Baby's First Haircut

When you were _____ old, _____ gave you your first haircut.

YOU

- ☐ Were scared and cried
- ☐ Kept trying to grab the scissors
- ☐ Kept turning to look, which was scary for us
- ☐ Couldn't care less
- ☐ Loved the attention
- ☐ Other: _____

WE FELT

- ☐ Excited to see your new look
- ☐ Worried about your curls not growing back
- ☐ Worried about you getting poked with the scissors
- ☐ Proud and surprised to see you growing up
- ☐ Other: _____

TAPE A LOCK OF HAIR
HERE OR ADD A BEFORE
AND AFTER PHOTO

Parents' Changing Style

MOMMY'S CHANGING STYLE

- [ ] Now she wears messy T-shirts and sweats.
- [ ] She got a bob or a mommy haircut
  so Baby wouldn't pull her hair.
- [ ] She rarely gets out of her pajamas.
- [ ] She still makes an effort to look nice.
- [ ] She stopped wearing dangly earrings.
- [ ] She looks pretty much the same except
  for spit-up stains.
- [ ] Other: _____

Details and thoughts: _____

_____

_____

_____

Did Dad change his style? _____

_____

_____

_____

_____

_____

After Baby was born, Dad didn't shave for _____
days/months.

First Attempts at Potty Training

When and what we told you: _____

_____

_____

WERE YOU READY?

☐ Yes

☐ No

☐ Details: _____

_____

BRIBES AND INCENTIVES

☐ Stickers

☐ M&M's

☐ TV or tablet time

☐ Money or other presents

☐ A family vacation

☐ Special big-kid underwear

☐ For boys, target practice

☐ Other: _____

FIRST BIG-KID UNDIES

☐ Disney: _____

☐ Superhero: _____

☐ Sesame Street or educational: _____

☐ Other: _____

Details, thoughts, and potty stories: _____

_____

_____

_____

"Shiitake mushrooms!"

Parents' Potty Mouths

Ever let a curse word slip in the heat of a parenting moment? _____

Funny story? _____

_____

_____

_____

_____

_____

_____

_____

_____

_____

ACCEPTABLE PG CURSE WORDS TO USE INSTEAD

- ☐ Oh, poop!
- ☐ Oh, fudge!
- ☐ Oh, tartar sauce!
- ☐ Shiitake mushrooms!
- ☐ Cheese and rice!
- ☐ Shut the front door!
- ☐ Son of a blee-blob!
- ☐ Other: _____

Potty Training Predicaments

MOST DISGUSTING BATHROOM
YOU WERE CHANGED IN

☐ Train station
☐ Superstore
☐ McDonald's or other fast-food restaurant
☐ Porta potty
☐ Other: _____

Other potty training stories: _____

_____

_____

_____

Parental Potty Training Predicaments

Did you ever take the training potty with you? _____

Any major public mishaps? _____

_____

_____

False starts and stops: _____

_____

_____

Did you give potty training a try and realize your child wasn't ready? _____

_____

_____

"Adam and Eve had many advantages, but the principal one was that they escaped teething."

MARK TWAIN

Baby's First Tooth

Telltale signs that you were teething: _____

_____

_____

THESE THINGS HELPED YOU FEEL BETTER:

- [ ] Teething medicine on your gums
- [ ] Chewing on your own fingers
- [ ] A washcloth or binky from the freezer
- [ ] Frozen teething ring
- [ ] Chewing on Mommy's/Daddy's Finger(s)
- [ ] Regular teething ring
- [ ] An ice pop
- [ ] Other: _____

Favorite teething toy: _____

THE FIRST TOOTH IS HERE!

Date: _____

ADD A PHOTO OF
BABY'S FIRST TOOTH

The Painful Truth

So many of Baby's stages are wonderful, but are there any that scare you?

_____

_____

_____

_____

_____

_____

Is it hard for you to watch while Baby struggles to learn new things or experiences pain? How do you deal with it?

_____

_____

_____

_____

_____

_____

_____

_____

_____

_____

_____

Now That We're Three

Now that We're Three

Now that we're three, we couldn't imagine life without you. You're so full of _____ .

You love to _____ and you're a natural _____ .

Besides all that, you're a ton of fun. One of the cutest things you do is _____ _____ . You make us feel so _____ . We're turning into a real family and your stuff is turning up in every room. Now that you're a little older, you're starting to enjoy _____ _____ .

Once you saw a(n) _____ and were so amazed you _____ .

When we went to _____ you were so delighted you _____ .

You love to _____ with Mommy and one of your favorite things to do with Daddy is _____ _____ . As a family we enjoy _____ . One great memory we have together is _____ .

We never could have imagined how one little person could have such a wonderful impact on our lives. We're looking forward to a lifetime of memories and adventures together.

HABITS WE PICKED UP:

- [ ] We started calling each other Mommy and Daddy instead of by our names.
- [ ] Mommy started cutting up Daddy's food in little pieces.
- [ ] Your things began outnumbering our things and took over every room.
- [ ] We can't go out with friends without talking about you.

ADD A PHOTO
OF THE THREE OF US

ADD A PHOTO
OF THE THREE OF US

Now That We're Three

WHEN WE WERE TWO WE THOUGHT WE'D HAVE SO MUCH TO TEACH YOU, BUT EVERYDAY WE LEARN SOMETHING NEW FROM YOU.

WHEN WE WERE TWO, GETTING OUT OF THE HOUSE MEANT

- ☐ Throwing on a jacket and shoes
- ☐ Brushing hair
- ☐ Other: _____

NOW IT'S

- ☐ Like packing to go to outer space
- ☐ Just a little extra hassle but we're getting it down
- ☐ Other: _____

Our record for getting out of the house fast is: _____
_____

WHEN WE WERE TWO WE LIKED TO

- ☐ Sleep in on weekend mornings
- ☐ Get up early and see the sunrise
- ☐ Stay up to chat into all hours of the night
- ☐ Other: _____

NOW

- ☐ We're happy if you sleep until _____ a.m.
- ☐ We're happy to go back to bed for a morning nap when you take one
- ☐ We get to stay up chatting into all hours of the night because you're up anyway
- ☐ Other: _____

WHEN WE WERE TWO WE ENJOYED WATCHING

- ☐ Thrillers & action films
- ☐ Dramas
- ☐ Rom-coms
- ☐ Documentaries
- ☐ Other: _____

NOW WE'RE HAPPY

- ☐ Watching Disney
- ☐ Watching Nick Jr.
- ☐ Watching Sesame Street
- ☐ Napping or showering while you watch TV
- ☐ Other: _____

When we were two, our favorite restaurant was

_____

NOW THAT WE'RE THREE, OUR FAVORITE RESTAURANT IS

- ☐ _____
- ☐ Our dining room

We like it because _____

_____

_____

_____

_____

_____

_____

WHEN WE WERE TWO, WE SOMETIMES ARGUED ABOUT

☐ What to cook for dinner
☐ What movie to see
☐ Other: _____

NOW WE ARGUE ABOUT

☐ How to get Baby to sleep
☐ How much to spend on toys
☐ Other: _____

When you get older, we'll miss _____

_____

_____

_____

_____

_____

_____

_____

_____

_____

_____

"Motherhood: All love begins and ends there."

ROBERT BROWNING

A New Kind of Love

MOM

I love being a mom because _____

_____

BUT IT'S HARD TO ADJUST TO

- ☐ The long hours without pay
- ☐ The uncommunicative boss
- ☐ The lack of spontaneity
- ☐ The unorganized work environment
- ☐ The sleep-deprivation
- ☐ Having less one-on-one time with Dad

As well as _____

DAD

I love being a dad because _____

_____

BUT IT'S HARD TO ADJUST TO

- ☐ The schedule
- ☐ The lack of downtime
- ☐ Favoritism
- ☐ The heavy workload
- ☐ All those dirty diapers
- ☐ Having less one-on-one time with Mom

As well as _____

First Realizations

MOM

First time I realized he would make a great dad:

_____

_____

_____

First time I stood back and saw him as a loving father:

_____

_____

_____

_____

DAD

First time I realized she would make a great mom:

_____

_____

_____

First time I stood back and saw her as a beautiful mother:

_____

_____

_____

_____

MOM

First time I stepped back and saw myself as part of a family: _____
_____
_____
_____

What I love most about being part of a family: _____
_____
_____
_____
_____
_____
_____

DAD

First time I stepped back and saw myself as part of a family: _____
_____
_____
_____

What I love most about being part of a family: _____
_____
_____
_____
_____
_____
_____

*"A hundred hearts would be too few
to carry all my love for you"*

AUTHOR UNKNOWN

Falling in Love with You

Here are some of the most adorable things you do that
make our hearts burst with love:

_____

_____

_____

_____

You are special because _____

_____

_____

_____

_____

And you're so loveable because _____

_____

_____

_____

_____

> "Making a decision to have a child . . . is to decide forever to have your heart go walking outside your body."
>
> ELIZABETH STONE

Falling in Love with Family

Forget "three's a crowd." Things we love to do all together:

_____

_____

_____

_____

_____

_____

Our family is special because _____

_____

_____

_____

_____

_____

_____

_____

_____

"I love thee with the breath, smile, tears of all my life!"

ELIZABETH BARRETT BROWNING

They Bring Out the Best

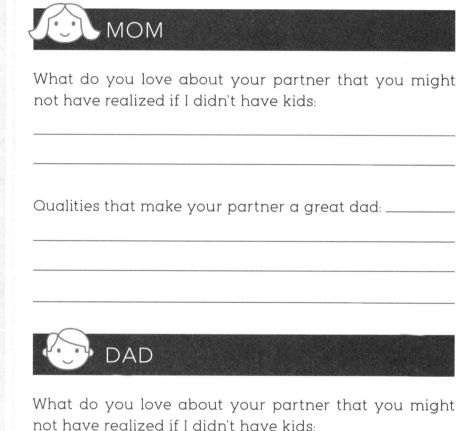

MOM

What do you love about your partner that you might not have realized if I didn't have kids:

_____

_____

Qualities that make your partner a great dad: _____

_____

_____

_____

DAD

What do you love about your partner that you might not have realized if I didn't have kids:

_____

_____

Qualities that make your partner a great mom: _____

_____

_____

_____

> "Grow old along with me! The best is yet to be."
>
> ROBERT BROWNING

MOM

Original, creative, funny, or kind things your partner does with Baby that you find adorable, charming, or sweet: _____

_____

_____

Original, creative, or funny thing that you love to do with Baby: _____

_____

_____

DAD

Original, creative, funny, or kind things your partner does with Baby that you find adorable, charming, or sweet: _____

_____

_____

Original, creative, or funny thing that you love to do with Baby: _____

_____

_____

*"If I had a flower for every time I thought of you . . .
I could walk through my garden forever."*

ALFRED LORD TENNYSON

Romantic Surprises

Describe a moment that was sweet or romantic between you and your partner while you were doing an activity as a family:

_____

_____

_____

_____

_____

_____

For some, cleaning up spit-up doesn't really qualify as romantic. Record some especially unromantic moments:

_____

_____

_____

_____

_____

_____

_____

Holding On to Moments

 **MOM**

What do you want to hold on to about this time in your life? _____
_____
_____

What precious moments with Baby do you want to remember forever? _____
_____
_____

What are you looking forward to doing with Baby in the future? _____
_____
_____

DAD

What do you want to hold on to about this time in your life? _____
_____
_____

What precious moments with Baby do you want to remember forever? _____
_____
_____

What are you looking forward to doing with Baby in the future? _____
_____
_____

Family Fun at Home

We loved staying around the house and doing these things together:

1. _____
2. _____
3. _____
4. _____
5. _____

Special memories: _____

_____

_____

_____

_____

_____

Fun Family Outings

Here are some fun family outings we had.

1. _____
2. _____
3. _____
4. _____
5. _____

Special memories: _____

_____

_____

_____

_____

_____

Fun One-on-One

FAVORITE MOMMY-BABY ACTIVITIES

Activity: _____

Activity: _____

Activity: _____

Other Mommy-Baby favorites: _____

_____

_____

_____

_____

_____

FAVORITE DADDY-BABY ACTIVITIES

Activity: _____

Activity: _____

Activity: _____

Other Daddy-Baby favorites: _____

_____

_____

_____

_____

_____

Mommy and Daddy Time

"Happiness is not an ideal of
reason but of imagination."

IMMANUEL KANT

What Makes a Date?

MOM

Before the baby, my idea of a date was _____
_____

Now, it's _____
_____

I can't wait until we can _____ again.

DAD

Before the baby, my idea of a date was _____
_____

Now, it's _____
_____

I can't wait until we can _____ again.

First Home Date

WHAT DID YOU DO AND WHAT MADE IT SPECIAL?

- ☐ Made popcorn and watched a movie
- ☐ Dressed up and ordered takeout
- ☐ Had a picnic in bed
- ☐ Lit candles
- ☐ Actually had a conversation
- ☐ Other: _____

Was it planned or spontaneous? _____

_____

_____

_____

_____

CHALLENGE: SEE HOW LONG YOU CAN LAST WITHOUT TALKING ABOUT BABY.

STAY-AT-HOME DATES AND WHAT MADE THEM SPECIAL

Date #1: _____

_____

Date #2: _____

_____

Date #3: _____

_____

Date #4: _____

_____

> "Remember tonight, for it is
> the beginning of always."
>
> DANTE

Romance Reinvented

FIRST LEAVE-THE-HOME DATE

Wow. What'd you do? _____

_____

_____

_____

_____

How did you feel? _____

_____

_____

_____

How long did it last? _____

Who wanted to call home to check on Baby first?

_____

_____

Details and thoughts: _____

_____

_____

_____

> "The best laid schemes of mice
> and men often go awry."
>
> ROBERT BURNS

Romance Gone Awry

Describe a time your romantic plans were foiled by unforeseen circumstances:

_____

_____

_____

_____

How did you handle it? _____

_____

_____

_____

_____

What did you learn from it? _____

_____

_____

_____

_____

_____

_____

Major Dates
and I Can't Waits

First holidays, birthdays, and more

Major Dates and I Can't Waits

How did you get so _____!

When you were born, you couldn't even _____

_____, and now you're

_____.

When you turned one your favorite thing in the world was

_____, and you could

_____ and _____

_____. You had

the most adorable smile with _____ teeth! Your first

birthday was _____

_____.

Holidays are _____ with you. So far, your favorite

holiday is _____. We think that's

because _____ _____.

We're so delighted with all your new tricks and talents

including _____, _____, and

_____, and how everyday you're more and more

_____

_____.

If we had one special thing to tell you as you're growing up, it

would be _____

_____

_____. And the other thing

we can't forget to tell you is how happy we are that you're ours.

ADD A PHOTO FROM A
FAVORITE CELEBRATION

ADD A PHOTO FROM A
FAVORITE CELEBRATION

ADD A PHOTO FROM A
FAVORITE CELEBRATION

> "The more you praise and celebrate your life,
> the more there is in life to celebrate."

OPRAH WINFREY

Baby's First Celebrations

Did you welcome Baby into the world with any formal party or celebration? _____

What was it? _____

Where was it held? _____

Who came? _____

_____

Did Baby even notice? _____

Any fun gifts? _____

_____

_____

What did Baby wear? _____

_____

_____

Details, thoughts, or stories: _____

_____

_____

_____

_____

_____

_____

_____

_____

_____

_____

_____

ADD A PHOTO
OF BABY

ADD A PHOTO OF
BABY AND FAMILY

Mama's First Mother's Day

Congrats, you've earned your own holiday!

MOM

MOTHER'S DAY FANTASY

- ☐ Flowers
- ☐ An outing with friends
- ☐ Sleeping late
- ☐ A brand-new car
- ☐ Breakfast in bed
- ☐ Being taken to brunch or dinner
- ☐ Other: _____

REALITY CHECK:

This is what really happened: _____

_____

_____

_____

What Mother's Day means to you: _____

_____

_____

Details on Mom's second Mother's Day: _____

_____

_____

_____

_____

Daddy's First Father's Day
Congrats, you've earned your own holiday!

	DAD

DADDY'S DAY FANTASY

- ☐ Golf clubs
- ☐ Sleeping late
- ☐ A day out with the guys
- ☐ Breakfast in bed
- ☐ A brand-new car
- ☐ Being taken to brunch or dinner
- ☐ Other: _____

REALITY CHECK:

This is what really happened: _____

_____

_____

_____

What Father's Day means to you: _____

_____

_____

Details on Dad's second Father's Day: _____

_____

_____

_____

_____

We're having a party!

Baby's first holidays: _____

_____

_____

CHRISTMAS, HANUKKAH,
OR OTHER WINTER CELEBRATION

How did you celebrate? _____

_____

Any new family traditions? _____

_____

Did Baby like opening presents? _____

_____

_____

_____

_____

NEW YEAR'S EVE OR NEW YEAR'S DAY

TOP 5 FAMILY RESOLUTIONS

1. _____
2. _____
3. _____
4. _____
5. _____

Did you do anything special? _____
_____

Did you stay up until midnight? Did Baby? _____
_____

HALLOWEEN

Baby's costume: _____

Did Mom and Dad dress up? _____

Did you decorate? _____

How did you celebrate? _____
_____
_____

Other favorite holidays and family gatherings:
_____
_____

Baby at One

(FEEL FREE TO ANSWER IN ONE WORD.)

Weight: _____   Length: _____

Baby's personality: _____

Baby loves _____

Baby hates _____

Achievement(s): _____

_____

_____

Unforgettable moment(s): _____

_____

_____

_____

ADD A PHOTO OF
BABY AT ONE

"We are not the same persons this year
as last; nor are those we love."

WILLIAM SOMERSET MAUGHAM

Parents When Baby Is One

MOM

How have you changed? _____

_____

_____

What about being a mom surprises you most?

_____

_____

_____

DAD

How have you changed? _____

_____

_____

What about being a dad surprises you most?

_____

_____

_____

"How do I love thee? Let me count the ways."

ELIZABETH BARRETT BROWNING

Baby Loves

Music: _____

_____

_____

Books: _____

_____

_____

Food: _____

_____

_____

People—real, imaginary, or on TV: _____

_____

Animals—plush, breathing, or on TV: _____

_____

Activities: _____

_____

_____

Other: _____

_____

We can't stop bragging about how you: _____

_____

_____

_____

_____

_____

⏱ TIME CAPSULE

If Baby could put all his or her favorite stuff in a time capsule, what would he or she pack?

_____

_____

_____

_____

_____

_____

_____

_____

_____

_____

_____

_____

_____

> "There is only one pretty child in the world, and every mother has it."

CHINESE PROVERB

Baby's First Birthday

What did you do? _____

_____

_____

Who came? _____

_____

_____

Triumph or disaster? _____

_____

_____

Feelings: _____

_____

_____

ADD A PHOTO OF
BABY'S FIRST BIRTHDAY

A Letter to Baby at One

Dear _____,

_____

_____

_____

_____

_____

_____

_____

_____

_____

_____

_____

_____

_____

_____

_____

_____

_____

_____

_____

_____

_____

Baby at Two

(Feel free to give two-word answers.)

Weight: _____   Length: _____

Baby's personality: _____

Baby loves _____

Baby hates _____

Achievement(s): _____

_____

_____

Unforgettable moment(s): _____

_____

_____

_____

ADD A PHOTO OF
BABY AT TWO

Parents When Baby Is Two

MOM

How have you changed? _____
_____
_____

What do you love about being a mom? _____
_____
_____

Highlights: _____
_____
_____

DAD

How have you changed? _____
_____
_____

What do you love about being a dad? _____
_____
_____

Highlights: _____
_____
_____

143

Baby Loves

Music: _____

Books: _____

Food: _____

People—real, imaginary, or on TV: _____

Animals—plush, breathing, or on TV: _____

Activities: _____

Other: _____

We can't stop bragging about how you _____

_____

⏱ TIME CAPSULE

If Baby could put all of his or her favorite stuff in a time capsule, what would he or she pack?

_____

_____

_____

_____

_____

Baby's Second Birthday Party

What did you do? _____

_____

_____

Who came? _____

_____

_____

Triumph or disaster? _____

_____

_____

Feelings: _____

_____

_____

_____

_____

ADD A PHOTO OF
BABY'S SECOND BIRTHDAY

A Letter to Baby at Two

Dear _____ ,

_____

_____

_____

_____

_____

_____

_____

_____

_____

_____

_____

_____

_____

_____

_____

_____

_____

_____

_____

_____

_____

> "The Bird of Time has but a little way to flutter."
>
> RUBAIYAT OF OMAR KHAYYAM

Two, Plus—I Can't Wait

MOM

MOMENTS I LOOK FORWARD TO:

1. _____
2. _____
3. _____
4. _____

Thoughts and feelings: _____

_____

_____

_____

DAD

MOMENTS I LOOK FORWARD TO:

1. _____
2. _____
3. _____
4. _____

Thoughts and feelings: _____

_____

_____

_____

"When you look at your life, the greatest happinesses are family happinesses."

DR. JOYCE BROTHERS

Memories and Milestones

SO MANY FUN, PRECIOUS MEMORIES, AND SO MANY MORE ON THE WAY. USE THIS SPACE TO LOOK BACK OR LOOK FORWARD.

_____

_____

_____

_____

_____

_____

_____

_____

_____

_____

_____

_____

_____

_____

_____

_____

You'll always be our baby.

USE THESE PAGES FOR MORE PHOTOS, LETTERS, AND MEMORIES.

Acknowledgments

A special thanks to some special people who helped me in this process, many of whom are invaluable in my life: My husband and partner, Allan Molho; my children, Willa and Nicky; my mom, Myrna G. Weiner (read: Magical Genie), and dad, Sy Weiner; Rudy and Roz Molho; Adam F. Weiner, David B. Weiner, Abby Phillipson, Eric Molho, Stacy Pettit, and the rest of my family, who are always funny and always there for me; my writer's group with endless patience: Sonia Jaffe Robbins, Maureen Hossbacher, Stacie Evans; my agent, Linda Konner; from Cedar Fort, Haley Miller, Whitney Lindsley, and Angela D. Baxter; and these wonderful friends, editors, and armchair editors: Rochelle Klempner, Rachel Meyers, Joni Schoonmaker, Barbara Aria, Fabienne Peyrat, Robin Halloran, Jessica Weigmann, Suzanne Keating, Kate Weil, Jennifer Rossi-Katz, Bob Eckstein, Suzanne Rust, Maite Castillo, Kerry Dziubek, Patti and Hiren Patel and Suzy Nguyen, as well as Charles Brennan, Marc J. Block, and Michael Ackerman, who swept in when needed with great advice.

About the Author

Jill Caryl Weiner has written on a broad range of parenting and education-related subjects from homeschooling and kids playing chess for the *New York Times* and the *Wall Street Journal* to innovative educational apps and decorating a pregnant belly for *Time Out New York Kids* and Mom365. Besides writing about parenting and education, she writes regularly about people, sports, and New York City for a variety of publications and websites.

In 1999 her life was blown apart—in a good way—when her first child was born. Not only did she have to take care of a seemingly alien life-form while trying to keep up her freelance writing career, but her spontaneous relationship with her husband was also sideswiped. At that time, a journal like *When We Became Three* would have been a life raft: fostering communication with her husband, offering a lighthearted perspective on parenting, and providing an honest, fun, multilayered book to record their memories in.

Jill lives in New York with her husband and two children.

To learn more about Jill and her writing, visit her website: www.jillcarylweiner.com.